Moroccan Cookery

Step by step illustrations

Moroccan Salad

- 1 green pepper	*- 1 tablespoon oil*
- 2 tomatoes	*- 1 teaspoon vinegar*
- 1 cucumber	
- 1 small onion	***Decoration:***
- salt , black pepper	*some black olives*

Method

Wash and peel vegetables. Cut them into small dices then combine in a salad bowl.

Vinegar dressing (French dressing)

Mix together oil, vinegar, salt and pepper. Pour the dressing over the salad, mix well. Garnish with black olives diced.

Bakkoula Salad (Mallow Salad)

- 2 bunches bakkoula(mallows)
- ½ glass olive oil
- 1 teaspoon cumin
- 1 teaspoon paprika
- 1 teaspoon Cayenne pepper
- salt
- 5 garlic cloves
- 1 bowl chopped parsley and coriander
- 1 lemon juice
- 50g red olives
- 1 preserved lemon

Method

Cleanse bakkoula bunches and remove yellow and dead leaves. Rinse many times under stream of water. Drain and chop finely with a knife.

Steam the bakkoula in a couscous steamer for 20min.
Place it in a pan; add olive oil, cumin, paprika, Cayenne pepper, salt, and garlic lightly chopped parsley and coriander.

Fry gently over low heat 10min.Stir with wooden spatula, spraying lemon juice when cooked. Before serving garnish with red olives and strips of preserved lemon.

The same recipe could be prepared with spinach.

Zaalouk

- *2 medium eggplants*
- *salt, black pepper*
- *4 garlic cloves*
- *4 tomatoes*
- *5 tablespoons olive oil*
- *½ teaspoon paprika*
- *½ teaspoon cumin*
- *1 tablespoon parsley and coriander chopped*

Method

Peel eggplants, cut roughly, salt then poach with garlic over low heat. Drain and preserve.

Hull, blanch and de-seed tomatoes. Cut into pieces and cook in pan with oil, cumin, paprika, salt and pepper. You may add can tomato to thicken sauce and bring out taste.

Once sauce reduced, add parsley, coriander, eggplant cubes and garlic. Crash them when smooth with a wooden spatula until homogenous. Serve warm.

Pepper Taktouka

- *1 red pepper*
- *1 green pepper*
- *4 tomatoes*
- *5 tablespoons olive oil*
- *4 garlic cloves*
- *½ teaspoon paprika*
- *½ teaspoon cumin*
- *salt, pepper*
- *1 tablespoon parsley and coriander chopped*

Method

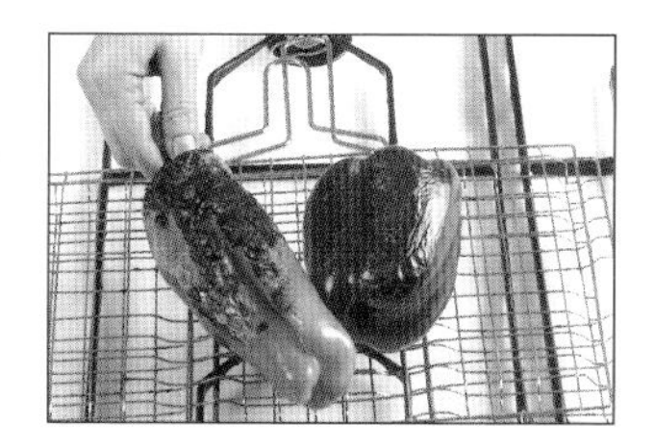

Toast peppers, preserve in plastic bag a few minutes so that they become easy to peel. (It's inadvisable to wash them after peeling). Dice peppers.

Hull, blanch and de-seed tomatoes then dice and fry quickly in a pan with oil, crushed garlic, paprika, cumin, salt and pepper. Reduce sauce over low heat, stirring.

Add to the sauce diced peppers and stir with a woodenspatula.Attheend,sprinkletacktoukawith parsley and coriander chopped as a decoration. Serve hot or cold as you wish.

Cucumber Salad

- *250g cucumbers*

Sweet sauce

- *2 tablespoons castor sugar*
- *1 tablespoon orange-flower water*
- *2 tablespoons lemon juice*
- *1 orange juice*
- *½ teaspoon oregano*

Salted sauce

- *salt and pepper*
- *2 tablespoons vinegar*
- *2 tablespoons oil*

Method

Wash and finely grate cucumbers.

For sweet salad

Add sugar, orange-flower water, lemon juice, orange juice, mix everything and sprinkle oregano.

For salted salad

Add to cucumbers salt pepper vinegar and oil, mix and serve.

Beetroot Salad

- *250g beetroots*

Salted sauce

- *2 crushed garlic cloves*
- *1 teaspoon vinegar*
- *salt and pepper*
- *1 tablespoon parsley finely chopped*

Sweet sauce

- *1 lemon juice*
- *2 tablespoons castor sugar*

Method

Poach beetroots until total cooking. Leave to cool, peel and dice.

For salted salad

Mix beetroots with garlic, vinegar, parsley, salt and pepper. Serve cold.

For sweet salad

Marinate beetroots into lemon juice and sugar for 5minutes, Mix and serve cold.

Potatoes Salad

- *250g potatoes*
- *salt*
- *1 teaspoon mustard*
- *2 tablespoons oil*
- *1 tablespoon vinegar*
- *¼ teaspoon white pepper*
- *1 tablespoon parsley finely chopped*
- *1 tablespoon diced onion*

Method

Wash and poach potatoes in salted water. Peel and roughly dice.

Sauce preparation

Mix mustard, oil, vinegar, white pepper, parsley and onion. Whisk well to obtain thick sauce.
Lay potatoes in a serving plate and spray with sauce. Serve cold.

Carrots Salad

- *250g carrots*
- *salt and pepper*
- *3 finely chopped garlic cloves*
- *2 tablespoons oil*
- *¼ teaspoon cumin*
- *1 tablespoon parsley finely chopped*

Method

Peel and cut carrots into small pieces, poach in salted water. Drain and put them in a pan, salt and pepper over low heat, then mix with garlic, oil cumin and parsley.
Serve hot or cold depending on the season.

Maakouda (Egg and Potato Fritters)

- *4 diced potatoes*
- *2 eggs*
- *2 tablespoons parsley and coriander chopped*
- *3 garlic cloves*
- *1 tablespoon cumin*
- *¼ teaspoon curcuma*
- *salt and pepper*
- *flour*

Method

Wash and poach potatoes in salted water then mash either with a fork or a mashing tool.

Place potato puree in a salad bowl; add 1 egg, parsley, coriander, crushed garlic, cumin, curcuma, salt and pepper. Mix well.

Make balls out of potato puree and flatten lightly with your fingers. Dip one at a time in 1 beaten egg then into flour. Take care of rubbing excess of flour out of maakoudas.

Fry maakoudas in hot oil and brown both sides.

Dried Peas Soup

- *500g dried peas*	- *water*
- *½ teaspoon salt*	- *olive oil*
- *1 teaspoon cumin*	- *Cayenne paprika*
- *8 crushed garlic cloves*	- *1 teaspoon paprika*

Method

Pour 1.5litres water in a pressure cooker and boil. Clean dried peas, wash and put them in hot water. Add salt, cumin and garlic. Cover and cook for 30min or until dried peas are completely cooked. Remove from heat, let it cool and process until you get a thick soup.
Reheat soup and serve, sprinkling paprika and Cayenne paprika. Add olive oil if you wish.

Dried Broad Beans Soup

- *500g dried broad beans*
- *water*
- *8 crushed garlic cloves*
- *1 teaspoon salt*
- *1 teaspoon paprika*
- *1 teaspoon cumin*
- *olive oil*
- *some paprika*

Method

Pour 1.5litres water in a pressure cooker and boil. Clean dried broad beans and pour into hot water, add crushed garlic cloves, salt, paprika and simmer 30min. Once dried broad beans cooked, remove from heat and cool. Process until thick soup. Reheat over low heat.
Serve hot, sprinkling paprika, cumin and adding olive oil.

Harira Soup

- ½ bowl lentils
- 1 bowl chick-peas
- 1 bowl diced meat
- 1 bowl chopped onion
- 1 bowl blanched and crushed tomatoes
- ½ bowl sticks of celery chopped
- 1 teaspoon ground ginger
- 1 pinch saffron
- 1 teaspoon butter or 1 teaspoon rancid butter
- salt
- ½ teaspoon pepper

- 2 litres water + 1 bowl water
- 1 bowl flour
- 50g tomato puree
- ½ bowl fine vermicelli
- 1 bowl parsley and coriander chopped

Method

Soak overnight lentils and chick-peas. Peel the later. Put in a pressure cooker lentils, chick-peas, diced meat, onion, tomatoes, celery, ginger, saffron and butter. Salt and pepper and add 2 litres water. Cook for 35min.

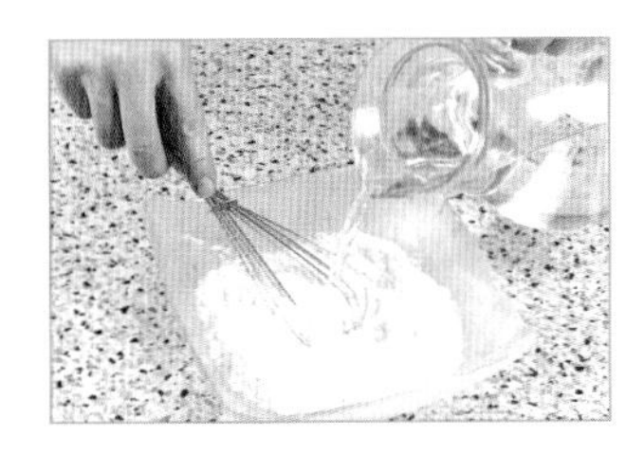

Liaison preparation
Dilute flour with water, whisking energetically to avoid lumps.

Verify that the meat is cooked, and then add can tomato. Mix well and pour liaison onto preparation. Stir constantly for 10min.

Add to the soup fine vermicelli, parsley and coriander. Stir and simmer one last time for 10min.
Serve hot.

Lentils

- 250g lentils (soaked overnight)	*- ¼ teaspoon pepper*
- 1 medium onion	*- some saffron*
- 1 large tomato	*- ½ teaspoon cumin*
- 4 crushed garlic cloves	*- 1 tablespoon parsley and coriander chopped*
- 1 tablespoon can tomato	*- water*
- ¼ glass olive oil	
- salt	

Method

Clean and wash lentils then put in a large pan. Add chopped onion, crushed tomato, garlic, can tomato, oil, salt, pepper, saffron, cumin and two big glasses water.

Put over moderate heat until complete cooking then add parsley and coriander chopped.

Serve hot.

Dried Beans

- *250g dried beans*
- *2 tomatoes*
- *4 crushed garlic cloves*
- *salt*
- *¼ teaspoon pepper*
- *some saffron*
- *½ teaspoon cumin*
- *¼ glass oil*
- *1 tablespoon can tomato*
- *1 tablespoon parsley and coriander chopped*
- *water*

Method

Soak overnight dried beans. Strain and poach in hot water. Strain and preserve. In a saucepan, put crushed tomatoes, garlic, salt, spices, oil, can tomato and two big glasses water. Boil over moderate heat. Add poached dried beans then chopped parsley and coriander. Simmer and remove from heat when beans become tender.

Serve hot.

Cockerel Stuffed with Semolina

- *2 cockerels*
- *3 crushed garlic cloves*
- *1 big onion*
- *¼ glass oil*
- *½ teaspoon salt*
- *½ teaspoon pepper*
- *½ teaspoon ginger*
- *some saffron*
- *1 and ½ big glass water*

Filling

- *1 bowl cooked and prepared semolina (see pages 32-33)*
- *2 tablespoons raisins*
- *3 tablespoons poached, peeled and crushed almonds*
- *½ tablespoon cinnamon*
- *1 tablespoon butter*
- *1 pinch gum Arabic powder*
- *1 tablespoon castor sugar*

Decoration: - *some poached and blanched almonds*

Method

Filling :
In bowl, put semolina, raisins, crushed almonds, cinnamon, butter, gum Arabic powder and sugar. Mix well all ingredients.

Wash cockerels with salted water, strain and stuff with semolina mixture. Weld openings with tooth-picks which you'll take off after cooking.

In a saucepan, place cockerels with chopped onion, oil, garlic, salt, pepper, ginger and saffron and seal over moderate heat.

Add poached and blanched almonds and 1 and ½ glass water. Cover and cook for 20min. Add water if necessary.
Serve cockerels hot with sauce.

Farmer Chicken

- *1 farmer chicken of 1.5kg*
- *¼ glass oil*
- *salt*
- *2 chopped onions*
- *4 chopped garlic cloves*
- *¼ teaspoon ginger*
- *¼ teaspoon pepper*
- *¼ teaspoon saffron*
- *a few of saffron pistils*
- *water*

Filling

- *1 packet Chinese vermicelli (100g)*
- *100g diced chicken livers*
- *2 crushed garlic cloves*
- *2 tablespoons parsley and coriander chopped*
- *salt and pepper*
- *2 tablespoons oil*

Decoration

- *100g red olives*
- *preserved lemon*

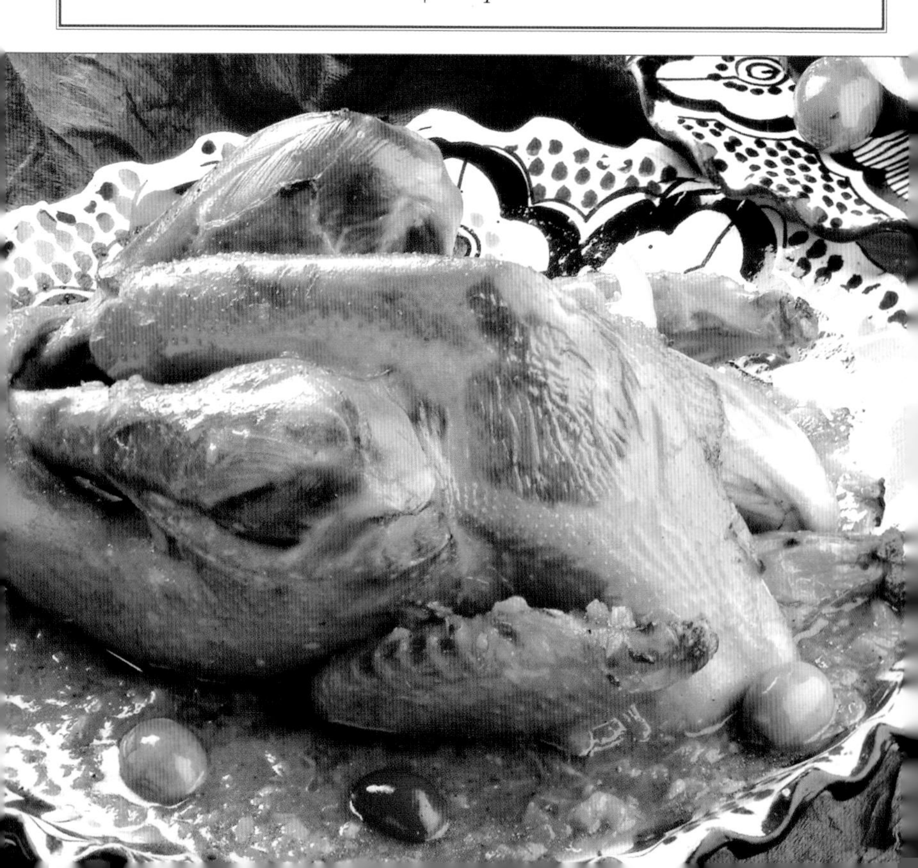

Method

Filling :
Soften Chinese vermicelli in a bowl of hot water for a few minutes. Strain and cut.

Add dices of chicken livers (giblets), crushed garlic, parsley, coriander, salt, pepper and 2 tablespoons oil. Mix well.

Wash chicken with salted water after preparing it. Stuff with vermicelli mixture then mend opening with a food thread.

Place chicken into a pressure cooker with oil, salt, chopped onion and garlic. Brown over moderate heat, stirring from time to time until golden elements. Add remaining spices, stir and pour 1.5litres water.
Cover and cook for about 1h.

Ten minutes before cooking, add red olives (method page 29).
Serve hot with sauce and decorate with strips of preserved lemon.

Chicken Pastilla

- *500g pastilla flaky pastry sheets*
- *200g butter*
- *1 egg yolk*

Filling
- *1 chicken of about 2kg*
- *5 medium onions chopped*
- *¼ glass oil*
- *1 teaspoon salt*
- *½ teaspoon pepper*
- *½ teaspoon cinnamon*
- *some saffron*
- *½ teaspoon saffron pistils*
- *water*
- *1 bunch parsley chopped*
- *8 eggs*
- *500g almonds (poached and blanched)*
- *200g castor sugar*
- *2 teaspoons orange-flower water*

Garnish
- *3 tablespoons honey*
- *100g almonds (poached, fried and crushed)*
- *cinnamon*
- *icing sugar*

Method

Wash chicken under stream of water and cleanse feathers' roots. In a saucepan, heat oil and seal chicken with chopped onions. Sprinkle salt, pepper, cinnamon and saffron.

Add saffron pistils, stir constantly until onions golden brown. Wet with 1litre water and boil for 30min over a brisk heat. 5min before end of cooking add parsley and stir. Remove chicken, bone and crumble flesh.

Keep saucepan over low heat to reduce sauce and add eggs one at time, stirring until homogenous mixture. Remove from heat when evaporated water.

Poach and blanch almonds. Golden in oil then drain onto absorbent paper. Leave it to cool a while then chop with sugar. Add orange-flower water to flavour almonds.

Brush a circular oven pan with melted butter and place 5 sheets in overlapping circles. They should overhang the edges of the pan. Brush with melted butter then place one sheet in the centre serving to contain filling.

Spread interior of pan with eggs and onions mixture and place chicken flesh as a second layer. Spray melted butter and spread almonds mixture as a third layer.

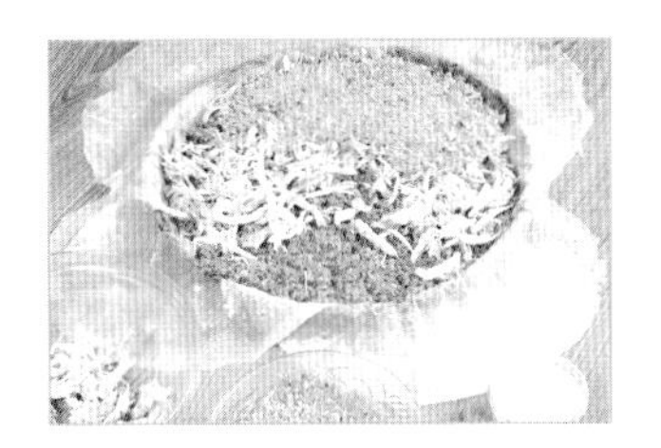

Turn up the overlapping sides of pastilla sheets onto filling and brush with melted butter. Put another sheet coated with egg yolk onto pastilla to seal surface and hide folds.
Coat one last time with melted butter and bake in preheated oven at 180° C for 30min. The pastilla should take golden color.

Before serving garnish pastilla with honey and sprinkle crushed almonds, icing sugar and cinnamon.

R'fissa

M'semmen *(Flat Cakes)*
- *2 bowls wholemeal flour*
- *1 bowl plain flour*
- *salt*
- *water*
- *1 bowl oil*

Chicken
- *1 chicken of 1.5kg*
- *2 big onions*
- *¼ glass oil*
- *1 bunch parsley and coriander*
- *salt and pepper*
- *½ teaspoon ginger*
- *some saffron*
- *a few saffron pistils*
- *water*

Decoration
- *200g fried and crushed almonds*

Method

Mix both flours with salt in a bowl and pour gradually water. Knead energetically until smooth dough. Add water if necessary.

Make little balls, brush with oil and flatten with your fingers to get small rounds.

Put one onto the other and seal by crushing the edges with your fingers.

Spread finely both sheets and brush with oil until you form one circular and almost transparent sheet.

Over low heat, cook the sheet onto a smooth pan lightly greased and brown both sides. Put it onto absorbent paper and do the same for the remaining balls.

Once you have finished cooking the whole dough, separate each beforehand sealed sheet to obtain many sheets.

Roll over and cut sheets, with scissors, into small pieces of 1cm thickness. Undo noodles then put them into a couscous steamer.

In the couscous saucepan put the chicken, chopped onions, oil, bunch of parsley and coriander, spices then salt and pepper. Seal chicken then add 2litres water. Cover and cook for 35min until chicken is cooked and leave some sauce to pour over m'semmen.

During the cooking of chicken remove cover and replace it with couscous steamer full of m'semmen pieces. Warm for 6min.

Serve putting the chicken in the middle of serving plate surrounded with m'semmen. Spray chicken stock sauce and sprinkle almonds.

Chicken with Olives

- *1 chicken of 1.5kg*
- *3 chopped onions*
- *¼ glass oil*
- *4 crushed garlic cloves*
- *salt and pepper*
- *½ teaspoon ginger*
- *some saffron*
- *water*
- *1 tablespoon parsley and coriander chopped*

Decoration

- *100g red olives*
- *some strips of preserved lemon*

Method

Rinse chicken with salted water and strain. Over moderate heat seal chicken in a pressure cooker with chopped onions, oil, garlic and salt. Stir well until coloured elements. Add spices and continue stirring until chicken is golden on all sides.

Add 1litre water, cover and cook for 30min. Verify if chicken is well done then remove it and brown in oven at 220° C. Preserve sauce.

Boil for 10 minutes red olives and drain.

Put olives into pressure cooker with strips of preserved lemon, parsley and coriander chopped and simmer until thick sauce.

Serve golden chicken with sauce and decorate with red olives and slices of preserved lemon.

Couscous with Vegetables

- *1.5kg meat*
- *1 onion*
- *½ glass oil*
- *½ glass olive oil*
- *1 tomato blanched and cut*
- *1 tablespoon salt*
- *1 teaspoon pepper*
- *1 teaspoon ginger*
- *¼ teaspoon saffron*
- *water (about 3litres)*
- *400g carrots*
- *250g turnips*
- *250g courgettes*
- *½ cabbage*
- *500g red pumpkin*
- *1 bunch parsley and coriander*
- *Cayenne paprika (if desired)*

Couscous

- *1kg semolina couscous*
- *4 tablespoons oil*
- *1 tablespoon salt*
- *water*
- *1 tablespoon butter or rancid butter*

<u>Method</u>

In a couscous saucepan and over moderate heat fry gently diced meat with oil then add chopped onion and tomato. Stir, salt, spice and once meat is golden, pour about 3litres water, cover and boil.

Wash and peel vegetables then cut in half lengthways.
Cut red pumpkin into large pieces and cabbage into two quarters. Re-wash vegetables with fresh water.

Meanwhile, put semolina couscous into a large plate; spray 2 tbsp oil and work between palms. Dilute salt in a big glass of water, moisten semolina then continue work. Leave it rest 20 min. and transfer semolina into the couscous steamer which you put over couscous saucepan. When steam rises over semolina, remove the steamer and cover saucepan.

Turn the couscous onto the large plate, spay a big glass of water and separate grains with your fingers then let it rest 10min.

During this time, add in the saucepan carrots, turnips, brunch of parsley and coriander then Cayenne paprika. Cook for second time semolina in the steamer for 20min. Semolina should be cooked over 3 times. Before the last cooking, add butter and work.

Before carrots and turnips are well done add red pumpkin, courgettes and cabbage. Cook for 15min. (These last vegetables cook quickly).

Put hot semolina in a serving dish and make a well in the centre. Put meat and vegetables all around. Spray with sauce and serve hot.

Tagine with Prunes

- *1kg of veal*
- *2 chopped onions*
- *¼ glass oil*
- *salt*
- *½ teaspoon pepper*
- *½ teaspoon ginger*
- *some saffron*
- *2 tablespoons castor sugar*
- *1 teaspoon butter*
- *½ teaspoon cinnamon*
- *a few saffron pistils*
- *4 crushed garlic cloves*
- *water*
- *250g dried prunes*

Decoration

- *1 tablespoon sesame seeds*
- *100g blanched and fried almonds*

Method

Over low heat seal meat with oil, onions chopped, salt, spices crushed garlic and stir occasionally.

Add 1 and ¼ litre water, cover and simmer until meat is done (for 40min), leaving some sauce for serving.

To preserve prunes, poach them and drain then put them into a saucepan over low heat. Add sugar, cinnamon and butter. Let it cook for 10min, stirring.

Serve hot and decorate with almonds and sesame seeds.

Tagine with String Beans

- *1kg beef*
- *1 onion*
- *¼ glass oil*
- *1 tomato peeled and diced*
- *4 crushed garlic cloves*
- *salt*
- *¼ teaspoon pepper*
- *½ teaspoon ginger*
- *1 pinch saffron*
- *water*
- *500g string beans*
- *2 courgettes*
- *1 tablespoon parsley and coriander chopped*
- *juice of ½ lemon*

<u>Method</u>

Over low heat brown pieces of beef with oil, chopped onion, tomato, garlic and salt. Stir and add spices to incorporate to all ingredients. Add water to the height of contents, cover and cook for 45min.

Remove strings from string beans and half-poach in salted water.
Drain and put them into saucepan after beef is cooked for 30min.

Wash, peel and cut courgettes. 10min before end of cooking put them into saucepan with lemon juice and parsley and coriander.

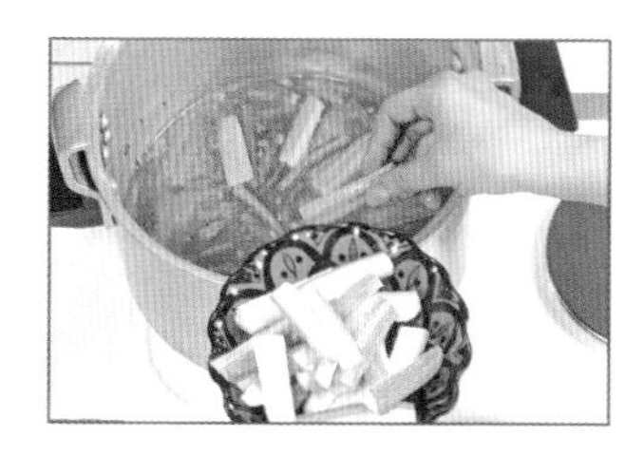

Serve hot with sauce.

Tagine with Artichokes and Peas

- *1kg meat*
- *1 onion*
- *4 crushed garlic cloves*
- *¼ glass oil*
- *salt and pepper*
- *some saffron*
- *½ teaspoon ginger*
- *1 peeled and diced tomato*
- *juice of ½ lemon*
- *water*
- *200g peas*
- *1kg artichokes*

Method

Seal meat in saucepan with oil, onion, salt, garlic and diced tomato. When onion sweats add spices then stir until golden mixture.

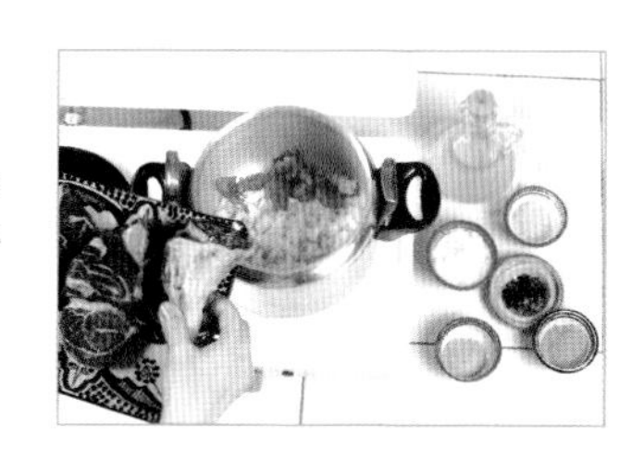

Add water necessary to cover all ingredients. Cover and cook over moderate heat for 30min.

Add peas and cook under cover for more 10min. Re-add water if necessary.

Thin out the leaves of artichokes, take off chokes and keep hearts in water with lemon juice added. Put them in saucepan and add lemon juice then simmer about 10 other min.

Serve hot with sauce.

Tagine with Quinces

- *1kg veal*
- *2 big onions*
- *¼ glass oil*
- *salt*
- *½ teaspoon pepper*
- *½ teaspoon ginger*
- *some saffron*
- *some saffron pistils*
- *4 crushed garlic cloves*
- *water*
- *500g quinces*
- *2 tablespoons castor sugar*
- *½ teaspoon cinnamon*

Decoration

- *a few blanched, fried and crushed almonds*

Method

In saucepan seal meat in oil then salt and add chopped onions. Incorporate spices and garlic, stir.

Once meat is brown, pour water to the height of meat. Cook over moderate heat for about 40min. Try to keep some sauce for presentation.

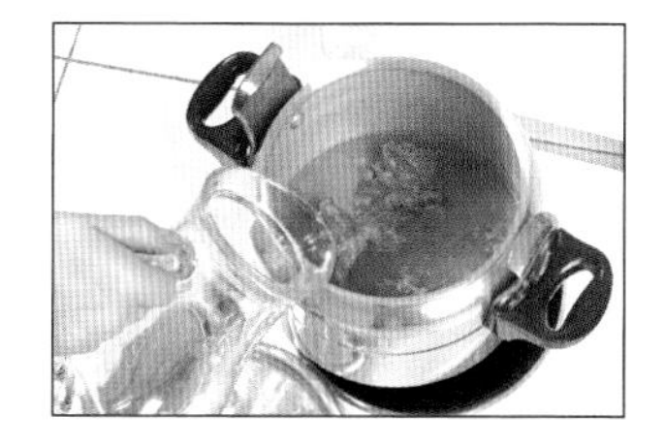

Wash, peel quinces, cut into equal quarters then put them into saucepan. Poach simply in water and drain.

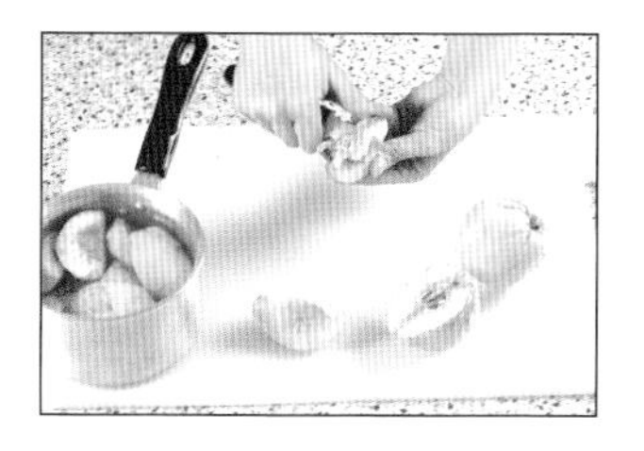

To preserve, keep saucepan over low heat and add sugar and cinnamon, stirring from time to time. After 15min remove from heat.

Serve tagine garnished with preserved quinces and crushed almonds.

Tagine with Cardoons

- *2 bunches cardoons*
- *750g veal*
- *¼ small glass oil*
- *1 onion*
- *salt*
- *¼ teaspoon pepper*
- *¼ teaspoon ginger*
- *some saffron*
- *4 garlic cloves*
- *water*

Decoration

- *red olives*
- *strips of 1 preserved lemon*

Method

Wash pieces of meat and brown in saucepan with oil, salt and chopped onion.
Stir until onion sweats and add spices and crushed garlic. Meat should be golden.

Pour water (necessary, it depends on how much sauce you want). Cover and cook for about 35min.

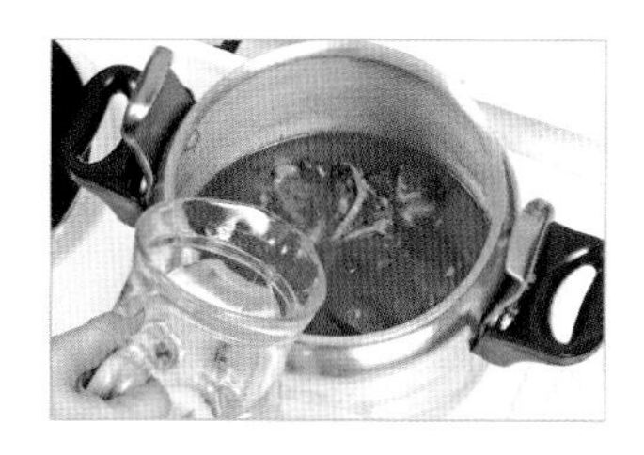

To clean cardoons, eliminate big extremities, very stringy, and keep only the interior without strings. Cut into small pieces and put them in water with lemon juice added. Drain and preserve.

Open saucepan, add cardoons and simmer until they become tender then add strips of preserved lemon and red olives.

For presentation, put first of all meat onto a serving dish then cardoons, garnish with strips of preserved lemon and red olives and then spray the sauce.

Leg of Mutton Stuffed

- *1 leg of mutton of 1.5kg*
- *3 tablespoons butter*
- *8 garlic cloves*
- *salt and pepper*
- *¼ glass oil*
- *1 big onion*
- *½ teaspoon ginger*
- *some saffron*
- *a few saffron pistils*
- *water*
- *1 teaspoon paprika*

Filling

- *250g minced lamb not seasoned*
- *150g diced liver*
- *1 egg*
- *1 big onion chopped and sweat*
- *2 crushed garlic cloves*
- *3 tablespoons parsley and coriander chopped*
- *½ teaspoon salt*
- *½ teaspoon ginger*
- *some saffron*
- *½ teaspoon paprika*
- *1 tablespoon butter*

Method

Finely bone the leg of mutton and coat inside with one tablespoon butter added to 3 crushed garlic cloves, salt and pepper.

Filling :
Mix well in bowl minced meat, liver browned beforehand in oil, egg, onion, garlic, parsley, salt, spices and one tablespoon butter.

Sew with food thread the leg leaving an opening for filling. Stuff well then mend to avoid filling from spilling out during cooking. Remove thread before serving.

In a pressure cooker, brown the leg of mutton into oil and one tablespoon butter, adding chopped onion, remaining garlic, salt pepper, ginger, saffron and saffron pistils.

Wet with water to the height of ingredients and cook for about 40min. Verify if meat is well done and remove from heat. Then put the leg of mutton onto a greased tray, brush it with butter added to paprika. Golden into oven at 200° C for 15 minutes.
Serve hot with vegetables.

Lamb Spleen Stuffed

- *4 lamb spleens*

Filling

- *350g minced meat*
- *5 tablespoons chopped coriander*
- *1 preserved lemon diced*
- *100g olives diced*
- *salt and pepper*
- *Cayenne paprika*
- *1 teaspoon cumin*
- *5 chopped garlic cloves*
- *2 onions chopped and sweat*

Sauce

- *1 big glass water*
- *1 onion*

Method

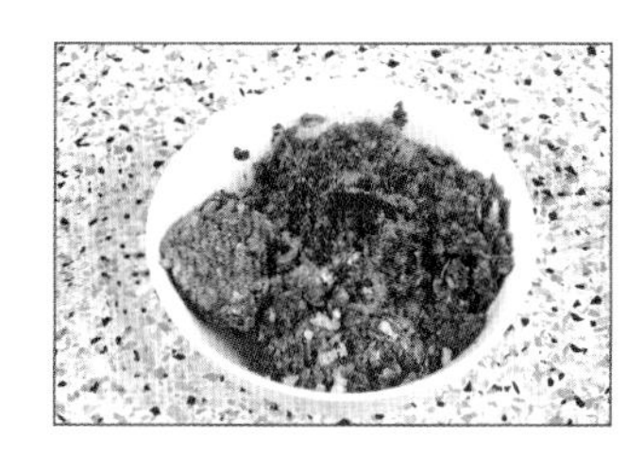

Filling :
In bowl mix minced meat, coriander, diced preserved lemon, diced olives, salt, pepper, Cayenne paprika, cumin, garlic and sweat onion.

Transfer filling into a piping bag and with a knife incise spleens and stuff them.

Once spleens stuffed, mend them or seal with toothpicks to avoid filling to spill out.
Prick spleens with a fork.

Put them in saucepan over moderate heat with chopped onion and big glass water. Simmer until well done, for 15 to 20min.

Serve hot.

Hargma (Calf's foot with Chick-peas)

- *1 calf's foot cut into pieces*
- *250g chick-peas (soaked overnight)*
- *1 big onion*
- *10 garlic cloves*
- *salt*
- *½ teaspoon pepper*
- *½ teaspoon ginger*
- *some saffron*
- *½ teaspoon cinnamon*
- *½ teaspoon paprika*
- *1 bunch parsley and coriander*
- *water*
- *a white and clean cloth*
- *250g wheat seeds*

Method

Wash pieces of calf's foot; put them into a pressure cooker with chick-peas, chopped onion, garlic, salt, spices and bunch of parsley and coriander. Pour water (2litres) and cook about 30min.

Put two tablespoons of washed wheat seeds in each piece of cloth, close and knot in shape of a purse. Do the same with remaining wheat seeds.

Soak purses into preparation and cook under cover for about 1hour.

Remove clothes before serving.

You may replace wheat seeds with rice or raisins.

Sea Food Pastilla

- *½ kg pastilla flaky pastry*
- *1 bowl melted butter*
- *1 egg yolk*

Filling
- *500g white fish*
- *500g shrimps*
- *400g squids*
- *½ packet black mushrooms (10g)*
- *2 packets Chinese vermicelli (100x2)*
- *2 big onions chopped and sweat*
- *4 tablespoons chopped parsley*
- *4 crushed garlic cloves*
- *1 teaspoon cumin*
- *salt and pepper*
- *½ teaspoon sweet paprika*
- *1 teaspoon Cayenne paprika*
- *1 preserved lemon diced*
- *6 tablespoons Soya sauce*
- *1 lemon juice*
- *150g grated cheese*
- *160g butter*
- *Chinese salt (optional)*

Garnish
- *150g grated cheese*
- *strips of preserved lemon*

<u>Method</u>

Cut into pieces white fish, salt and fry in 1 tablespoon butter.
Stir finely until well done. Preserve.

Shell and wash shrimps, salt and pepper then fry 5min into 1 teaspoon butter. Preserve.

Clean squids, wash and cut into rings. Strain, salt and pepper and fry 10min into 1 teaspoon butter. Preserve.

Tender black mushrooms into hot water, rinse then cut in tiny pieces and preserve. In another bowl, tender Chinese vermicelli in hot water. Cool, strain and cut into pieces. Preserve.

In a big pan and over moderate heat, brown into 1 teaspoon butter half portion of fish, shrimps, squids, sweat onion, parsley, mushrooms, Chinese vermicelli, garlic, cumin, both paprika, diced preserved lemon, soya sauce and lemon juice. Stir finely to incorporate all ingredients. Add salt if necessary.

Brush a round oven pan with melted butter and spread pastilla sheets in overlapping circles and overhanging the edges of pan. Brush them with melted butter. Place in the middle another pastilla sheet serving to contain filling.

Spread mixture over oven pan until uniform surface. Add remaining half of white fish and sprinkle the whole surface with grated cheese then spray with melted butter.

Turn up overlapping sheets onto filling and brush with melted butter. Put another sheet coated with egg yolk over pastilla to seal and hide folds. Brush one last time with melted butter and bake in preheated oven at 200° C for about 30min until golden pastilla.

When removed from oven, garnish with grated cheese and strips of preserved lemon.
Serve hot.

Stuffed Fish

- *1 fish of 1.5kg*
- *1 red pepper*
- *1 yellow pepper*
- *1kg fennel*
- *3 celery roots*
- *1 lemon*
- *2 tomatoes*
- *2 bay-leaves*
- *water*

Charmoula

- *5 tablespoons chopped parsley and coriander*
- *½ teaspoon salt*
- *½ teaspoon pepper*
- *1 teaspoon paprika*
- *1 teaspoon cumin*
- *some saffron*
- *juice of ½ lemon*

- *1 glass mixed oil with olive oil*
- *5 crushed garlic cloves*

Filling

- *130g rice*
- *½ teaspoon salt*
- *1 tablespoon butter*
- *2 tablespoons de-seeded olives*
- *1 small preserved lemon diced*
- *2 tablespoons oil*
- *2 tablespoons chopped parsley and coriander*
- *½ teaspoon paprika*
- *½ teaspoon pepper*
- *½ teaspoon cumin*

Method

Wash and cut vegetables into equal pieces to cook at the same time.

Filling :
Poach rice into salted water, strain and put it into bowl. Add butter, diced olives and preserved lemon, oil, parsley, coriander, paprika, pepper and cumin. Mix and preserve.

To prepare charmoula, you need to mix its ingredients.

Hollow out, scale and clip fish then wash under stream of water. Spread little of charmoula inside fish and stuff.
Mend with food thread. With a knife, score fish and coat with charmoula.

Onto an oven tray put vegetables as a bed, add bay leaves and put on stuffed fish. Then spray everything with remaining charmoula.
Decorate with red and yellow peppers and strips of preserved lemon, add 1glass water and bake into preheated oven at 180° C until vegetables are well done. (For about 30min).

Sardines Balls

- *1 kg sardines*
- *2 carrots*
- *2 potatoes*
- *2 tablespoons poached rice*
- *1 sliced lemon*
- *1 sliced tomato*
- *1 bay leaf*
- *water*
- *100g olives*

Charmoula *(Marinade)*
- *4 tablespoons chopped parsley and coriander*
- *½ teaspoon salt*
- *½ teaspoon pepper*
- *1 teaspoon paprika*
- *1 teaspoon cumin*
- *some saffron*
- *juice of 1 lemon*
- *½ glass oil and olive oil mixed*
- *1 tablespoon crushed garlic cloves*

Method

Charmoula
In bowl, mix chopped parsley and coriander, salt, pepper, paprika, cumin, saffron, garlic, mixed oils and lemon juice.

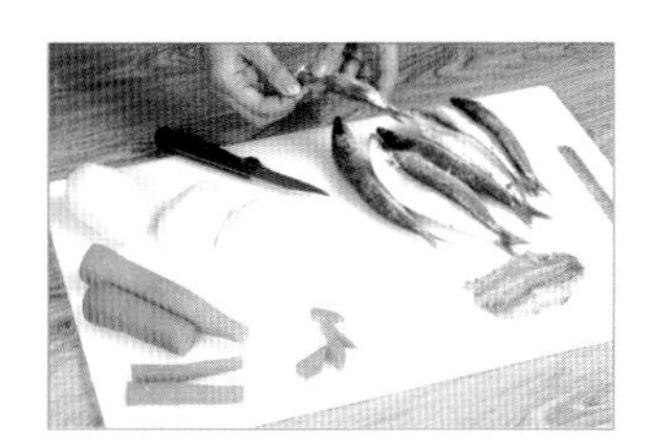

Wash and hollow out sardines then bone. Peel and cut carrots into small pieces. Do the same for potatoes.

Chop sardines in a mill (you may do it with your hands).

Mix half of charmoula with rice and chopped sardines then shape little balls.

Put balls into saucepan; add carrots, potatoes, lemon, tomato, olives, bay leaf and remaining charmoula.
Pour 2 glasses water, cover and simmer over low heat for about 15min.

Serve hot.

Seffa with Fine Vermicelli

- *1kg fine vermicelli*
- *½ glass oil*
- *salt*
- *water*
- *150g raisins*
- *2 tablespoons butter*

Decoration
- *100g poached, fried and crushed almonds*
- *icing sugar*
- *cinnamon*

Method

To steam fine vermicelli, boil 2litres water, with lemon juice added, into couscous saucepan. Then put fine vermicelli into flat and large plate, work with oil. Transfer them into couscous steamer and cook over moderate heat for about 20min.

Remove steamer and put again fine vermicelli into flat and large plate. Spray with 1 glass salted water, mix well and undo possible knots with your hands.
Put for second time vermicelli into steamer. Repeat until complete cooking of fine vermicelli.

Just before the last cooking step, add raisins, beforehand cleaned and rinsed, to vermicelli to steam with.

Before presentation, put fine vermicelli into flat dish, add 2 tablespoons butter, let it melt and mix.

Serve in a serving dish and decorate with crushed almonds, cinnamon and icing sugar.

Seffa with Rice

- 2 bowls rice
- 4 bowls water
- 3 tablespoons butter
- 1 tablespoon castor sugar

Para decorar:
- 100g almonds (boiled, blanched and fried)
- cinnamon
- icing sugar

Method

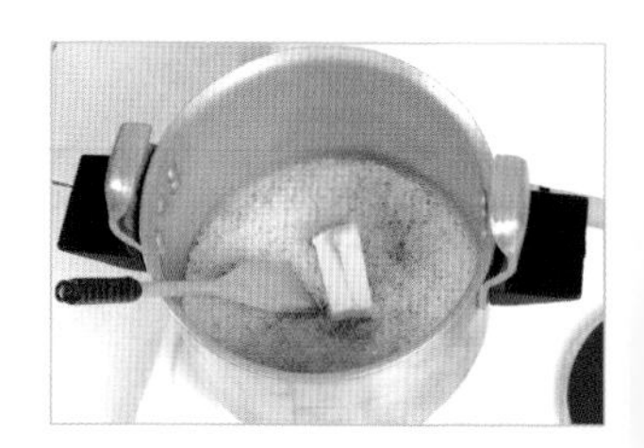

Put rice and butter into saucepan over low heat, stirring constantly.

Add water and cook until total absorption, stirring from time to time. Add sugar and let it melt.

For presentation, place into dish rice in a shape of a pyramid and decorate with almonds, icing sugar and cinnamon.

Briouates with Almonds

- *250g poached and blanched almonds*
- *100g castor sugar*
- *50g butter*
- *½ teaspoon cinnamon*
- *1 pinch gum Arabic powder*
- *1 tablespoon orange-flower water*
- *24 sheets of pastilla flaky pastry*
- *1 egg yolk*
- *oil to fry*
- *500g honey*

Decoration

- *50g fried and crushed almonds*

Method

Boil almonds, blanch, drain with clean cloth then mix with sugar. Add 1 teaspoon butter, cinnamon, gum Arabic powder and orange-flower water. Mix well with your hands then shape little balls.

Cut pastille sheets into strips, brush each one with melted butter and put inside a ball of almond paste. Fold in triangular shape going from right to left then from left to right. Seal last part of the strip with egg yolk.

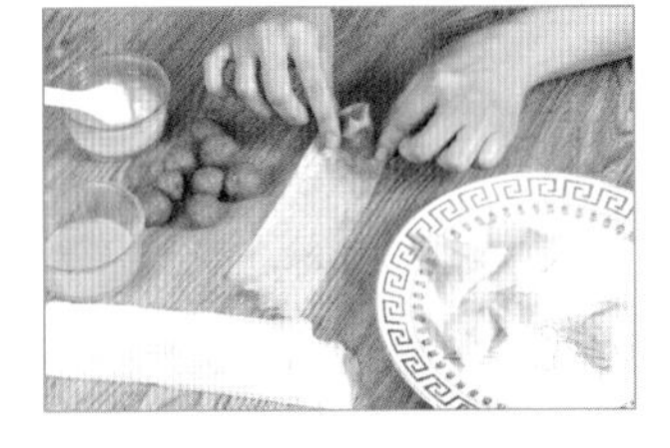

Golden briouates on both sides in hot oil then soak them into honey. Strain and decorate with crushed almonds.

Serve cold.

We may also boil almonds, blanch, fry and mix them with sugar, butter, cinnamon, gum Arabic powder and orange-flower water. Before frying, briouates can be kept in hermetic box in freezer.

Contents